The Bible History Of Satan: Is He A Fallen Angel?

A Cambridge Master Of Arts

In the interest of creating a more extensive selection of rare historical book reprints, we have chosen to reproduce this title even though it may possibly have occasional imperfections such as missing and blurred pages, missing text, poor pictures, markings, dark backgrounds and other reproduction issues beyond our control. Because this work is culturally important, we have made it available as a part of our commitment to protecting, preserving and promoting the world's literature. Thank you for your understanding.

THE

BIBLE HISTORY OF SATAN.

IS HE A FALLEN ANGEL?

BY A CAMBRIDGE MASTER OF ARTS.

LONDON:
THOMAS HATCHARD, 187 PICCADILLY, W.
1858.

London:—Printed by G. Barclay, Castle St. Leicester Sq.

THE BIBLE HISTORY OF SATAN.

IS HE A FALLEN ANGEL?

THIS title must not be thought strange nor its subject so clear and certain as to render examination superfluous; no doubt most men have given their assent to a theory which I cannot but think destitute of foundation, but they have done so for the most part without full inquiry, and, consequently, without genuine conviction; but, at any rate, true or false, the theory is one claiming the authority of inspiration, and, as such, well worthy of our most attentive consideration; and the object of the following pages is to test popular belief, by Scripture revelation, in reference to it.

To do this the more clearly, it will be necessary, at the outset, to state generally *what* that popular belief is; secondly, we must examine passages in the Apocalypse and elsewhere with a view to show that they are not to be applied literally to Satan, or if so, that they do not refer to his history at a period prior to the creation of man, before which time the Devil was what he is; thirdly, we must refer to some texts which tell of fallen angels, but those not Satan and his angels; fourthly, we shall come to the main object in view, viz. the history, nature, station, pursuits, power, and destiny of the Devil, so far as revealed in Scripture.

First, then, what is the popular idea of the Devil generally entertained, and supposed to be founded upon Scripture? Is it not this, that at one period Satan was a good angel; that, moved by pride, he rebelled against God, and was punished, with other subordinate angels, by being driven from heaven; that thereupon he commenced his too successful warfare against the souls of men? This is popular belief, and by that term I mean not only the belief of the vulgar, but, so far as I know, the belief also of every commentator on Holy Writ. But the question for our consideration is, what is the Bible history on the subject? In the tenth chapter of St. Luke, verse 18, our Saviour—but without any allusion, as has been suggested, to Isaiah, xiv. 12—says, " I saw Satan as lightning fall from heaven;" but this, as well as the account of the expulsion of Satan from heaven by Michael the Archangel (Rev. xii. 7), is figurative language, denoting the triumph of the religion of Christ over the kingdom of Satan. This is the universal interpretation, and yet it would appear that the *literal* signification of a text, universally held to have a *figurative* meaning only, has unwittingly paved the way for the reception of an idea nowhere taught in Scripture. But suppose a literal allusion, with or without the figurative application, still the event cannot establish as a fact that Satan was an angel of light, and fell from heaven previously to the fall of man; for our Saviour's vision, as well as St. John's, refers to a period subsequent to our Lord's advent, and therefore cannot account for Satan's state and position when he tempted Adam and Eve to their fall.

But let us examine our Saviour's vision a little in detail (St. Luke, x. 18), " I saw Satan as lightning fall from heaven." Doddridge explains this as of Christ seeing Satan's (supposed) fall from heaven on his first transgression, but it seems much more like a prophetic vision, in which he foresaw and foretold the destruction of Satan's kingdom by the preaching of the Gospel, of which, in fact, the seventy were now rejoicing in the first-fruits, and saying, " Lord, even devils are subject unto us through thy name." " Behold," our Saviour adds, " I will give you power to tread upon serpents and scorpions, and upon the whole power of the enemy," not only alluding to Satan as " the serpent," but literally to the serpent at Melita, and, figuratively, to the power given, by which His religion should survive the persecutions of its adversaries. The expression "fall from heaven," signifying only from great power and distinction, is not without its parallel in heathen writers. Thus, Cicero, "Collegam tuam de cœlo detraxisti," "You have pulled down your colleague from heaven;" and again Pompey is said, "Ex astris cecidisse," "to have fallen from the stars of heaven,"—in both cases meaning from a great height, but not from heaven any more than I believe our Saviour to mean that Satan fell from heaven. But I much doubt whether the expression is even so strong as it stands in our translation, whether it is not rather, "I saw Satan fall as lightning from heaven;" *that the lightning falls from heaven, not Satan*, but his fall was to be like it in rapidity and magnitude. Isaiah uses similar expressions: "How art thou fallen from heaven, O Lucifer, son of the morning!" (Isa. xiv. 12.) But this is no allusion to Satan, nor is it so considered by commentators, but applied to the King of Babylon.

Let us further examine St. John's account of the expulsion of Satan from heaven by Michael the Archangel. (Rev. xii. 7.) This is not a representation of actual war in heaven, as adopted by Milton and others, but of the conflict between Christianity and Heathenism, or Christianity and Popery: the former upheld by Michael, so frequently God's agent for the defence of His people; and the latter by Satan, the prince of this world and its wickedness. In Daniel, xii. 1, we read of Michael, "the great prince that standeth for the children of thy people;" and in a preceding chapter (Dan. x. 13), of the prince of the kingdom of Persia (no doubt the Devil exercising an evil power over Persia), withstanding Daniel twenty-one days, who is then aided by Michael. In St. Jude we find an allusion to Michael the Archangel contending with the Devil about the body of Moses. (Jude, 9.). In Zachariah (iii. 1), we have Joshua, the high-priest, standing before the angel of the Lord, and Satan standing at his right hand to resist him; a perpetual check given by God's Archangel to the devices and power of Satan,—devices and power so cunning and vast that angels might check, but Christ alone could ultimately destroy, and even Christ *only by His own death*, as we read (Heb. ii. 14), "Forasmuch then as the children are partakers of flesh and blood, he also himself took part of the same, *that* through death he might destroy him that had the power of death, *i. e.* the Devil." Next, let us examine the supposed incentive to Satan's rebellion against God— pride. Upon what is this idea grounded? St. Paul, in his Epistle to Timothy (1 Tim. iii. 6), says that a bishop "must not be a novice, lest being lifted up with pride he fall into the condemnation of the devil." Hence it has been assumed that by pride Satan fell from heaven; but if we study the original, the passage appears rather to signify "lest he expose himself to the censure of *the slanderer*," just as the word διαβόλος is used two verses afterwards, "Let not the women be διαβόλους," "slanderers" (1 Tim. iii.

11), meaning thereby the Jewish or heathen adversary of Christianity; for the Apostle goes on to say that he must have " a good report of them *which are without*," *i. e.* of the heathen or Jews; so in the ninth verse of Nehemiah, chap. 5,— " Ought ye not to walk in the fear of our God, because of the reproach (ὀνειδισμοῦ) of the heathen, our enemies ?"

If we compare 1 Tim. iii. 7 with 1 Tim. v. 15, I think we find some corroboration of this view of the question: 1 Tim. iii. 7—"Moreover, he must have a good report of them which are without, lest he fall into the reproach and snare of the *adversary*" (τοῦ διαβόλου); 1 Tim. v. 15—"Give none occasion to the *adversary* (τῷ ἀντικειμένῳ) to speak reproachfully (λοιδορίας χάριν)." Here we have the same sentiment expressed in different terms,— τῷ ἀντικειμένῳ—"the adversary"—in one case, seeming to illustrate and explain the word τοῦ διαβόλου—"the adversary"—in the other; and ὀνειδισμὸν—"reproach"—in the one, answering to λοιδορίας χάριν — "for reproach" — in the other. The article is prefixed in both cases; but if we consider how constantly and systematically a spy was set upon the actions, and introduced into the assemblies, of early Christians, that he might be able to slander or accuse (διαβάλλειν) them, we can scarcely be surprised to find the agent termed διάβολος, or to find him designated specially to his employment by the prefix of the article.

It has been remarked that, in the plural number

only, διάβολος is used in the sense of "slanderer" or "adversary;" but may not 1 Tim. iii. 6, 7, be instances to the contrary, as certainly is St. John, vi. 70, where διάβολος appears without the article, and is better translated "adversary" than "devil;" in fact, as rendered in our version, "a devil," the word requires to be resolved into its primitive meaning before we arrive at the sense of the passage—why is one "a devil?" because a devil means an adversary, and in this sense, one was "a devil." Moreover, Pindar uses ὁ διάβολος as a slanderer. In 2 Tim. ii. 26, we have ἐκ τῆς τοῦ διαβόλου παγίδος, this is rendered "from the snare of the devil;" hence it is argued, εἰς παγίδα τοῦ διαβόλου, a similar expression (1 Tim. iii. 7), must refer to the same being; but this does not follow, nor is it certain that, in 2 Tim. ii. 26, the Devil is intended. If the similarity of expression were to be held conclusive, then I might hold 1 Tim. v. 15 as conclusive against 1 Tim. iii. 7, indicating the Devil. But 2 Tim. ii. 26 is very difficult, and certainly, in some respects, improperly translated. Suppose διαβόλου here to mean "the Devil," then the translation should run thus—"and that they who were taken captive of him (the Devil) may arouse from the snare of the Devil to the will of Him (God);" but it may here also mean "the adversary," one of the ἀντιδιατιθεμένους mentioned in a previous verse, and the passage would run thus—"In meekness teaching the adversaries, in case God may give them repentance to the acknowledging of the truth, and that those who had been entrapped by him (the adversary— quære, to renounce their faith?), may arouse out of the snare of the adversary to the will of God"—but this is beside my argument. To return (1 Tim. iii. 7):—suppose διαβόλος in this place to mean "the Devil," it may be, "Lest he render himself liable (not to punishment for a fault similar to that of the Devil, but) to punishment *by* the Devil." This was the interpretation of St. Chrysostom and of Theodoret, and yet they appear to have overlooked the consequence,—viz., that there is no other ground for supposing Satan to have fallen *by pride;* but, be this as it may, the fall of Satan from heaven not being revealed, it is unreasonable to allege pride to have been the cause of that which may never have happened.

But not only is διαβόλος explained by ἀντικείμενος and ἀντιδιατιθέμενος; but κρίμα also, which in 1 Tim. iii. 6, has been made to signify the judicial sentence pronounced upon Satan, is illustrated by its use in a subsequent chapter (1 Tim. v. 12), ἔχουσαι κρίμα, which I take to mean "incurring the censure" of the same adversary, whose accusation St. Paul, in the next verse but one, exhorts them to avoid; and this adversary—not the devil, but the heathen or Jew—taking advantage of the lapses of professed Christians who had turned back after Satan (1 Tim. v. 15); and why not the same adversary as in 1 Tim. iii. 6, 7?

Thirdly,—we must refer to fallen angels mentioned in Scripture. It has always been a matter of doubt and difficulty with modern commentators to determine what was really intended by the narrative in the sixth chapter of Genesis. We read (Gen. vi. 2): "The sons of God saw the daughters of men, that they were fair, and took them wives of all they chose." Now who were these sons of God? who were these daughters of men? Most commentators have laid it down, and it has been very generally accepted, that by "the sons of God" we are to understand "the sons of Seth," as distinguished from those of Cain, and the "daughters of men," to be "the daughters of Cain," as distinguished from those of Seth; but the objections to this appear so strong, that, even without illustrating the passage by reference to the New Testament, it will appear much more rational (and doubtless as a general rule it is much safer) to follow the interpretation naturally suggested by the text. This was generally received in ancient times, and most ably insisted upon by at least one modern author (Maitland). Amongst the many arguments against the common interpretation, it will be sufficient for my purpose briefly to select a few of the most prominent, and to embody them in the form of interrogatories.

Why are the daughters of Cain supposed to have been pre-eminently fair? Whence did the sons of Seth come *down* to the daughters of Cain? Why (as the narrative goes on to relate) was the offspring of this connexion "*the Giants?*" It seems to me also an argument of considerable weight, that, in the sentence "daughters of men," it is, in the Hebrew, "the daughters of *Adam*." Now the word *Adam* is constantly used to designate the whole human race; but in no one instance is it applied to *a race of men*. In this passage it is most properly put in opposition to the sons of God, or angels, who were of a different nature; but if the sons of God are sons of Seth, and the daughters of men are daughters of Cain, both are the children of Adam, and, therefore, the appellation "Adamites" cannot but be improperly applied to one, if intended to distinguish it from the other.

But by following up Maitland's ideas, we shall clearly find that, if we accept the passage in its obvious and literal sense, and interpret "the sons of God" to signify angels, the difficulty will not only vanish, but we become possessed of a masterkey to some passages in the New Testament, which, without such a key, are apparently incapable of any satisfactory explanation. To proceed: We read (Gen. vi. 2): "The sons of God saw the daughters of men that they were fair, and took them wives of all which they chose." The angels of God conceived lust for the daughters of men, &c. &c.; but St. Jude (verse 6), speaking of the lusts of men, brings forward the example of angels, who were led away by their lusts, and therefore, probably, the example of the very angels mentioned in Genesis,—"and the angels which kept not their first estate, but left their own habitations, he hath reserved in everlasting chains, under darkness, unto the judgment of the great day:" but these cannot be Satan with his angels, who is not yet "in chains under darkness," but permitted in God's wisdom to be as "a roaring lion, that walketh about seeking whom he may devour.' 1 Pet. v. 8. But let us look also at the second Epistle of St. Peter. What does he say? (2 Pet. ii. 4), "For if God spared not the angels that sinned, but cast them down to hell, and delivered them into chains of darkness, to be reserved unto judgment," &c. &c. Here, again, in a discourse *upon the lusts of the flesh*, the fate of the same angels as those in St. Jude is referred to almost in the same terms; but in one respect, there is a difference, inasmuch as that, by the use of a single word, he gives the most extraordinary confirmation to the idea, that these fallen angels to which he alludes are the identical angels or sons of God, who saw the daughters of men that they were fair, &c. &c.

In Genesis the narrative proceeds, "And there were giants in the earth" (or rather, both in the Hebrew and in the Septuagint, "*The giants* were in the earth") "in those days, and also after that, when the sons of God came in unto the daughters of men, and they bare children unto them." The single word to which I allude is that which our translation renders "cast down to hell;" but in the original, a most remarkable word, $\tau\alpha\rho\tau\alpha\rho\omega\sigma\alpha\varsigma$, a word chosen for the occasion, and in the Bible used nowhere besides, derived from the Greek Τάρταρος, which by Greek authors is used for that place where the rebellious Titans were chained: but who were the Titans? They were the fabled offspring of Cœlus and Terra—demigods. And what is the word translated "giants?" Gen. vi. 4. In the Hebrew it is "Nephilim," or "the fallen ones," rendered in the Septuagint by the Greek word "Gigantes," which was the term applied to the fabled sons of Earth and Heaven—demigods.

Οὕς καλιοῦσι Γίγαντις ἐπώνυμον ἐν μακάρισσι
Οὕνικα γῆς ἐγένοντο καὶ αἵματος οὐρανίοιο.—*Orpheus.*

"Sprung from the earth and heavenly blood combined,
Among the gods the giants' name they find."

Hence we conclude "Nephilim" to have the like signification, and according to its derivation, the "Nephilim" were the sons of the *fallen* angels. Thus we have these extraordinary coincidences: in Genesis the offspring of the sons of God and the daughters of men is called by the same name as the heathen Titans. In St. Peter, the angels, the sons of God, the parents of the demigods or giants, are said to be imprisoned in a place, not called by the Scripture name signifying hell, but in heathen Tartarus, in that place where the heathen giants were said to be confined. What more is required to prove the connexion between the several places I have cited? What more to prove that the angels mentioned are not Satan and his angels? The angels of God, then, who sinned, were cast out of heaven, and kept in chains *to be judged* at the great day : do we meet with a reference to the same angels in the First Epistle to the Corinthians, where St. Paul says the saints shall judge them? "Know ye not that we shall judge angels?" (1 Cor, vi. 3.)

Is it venturing too much to suppose that the reason why they were to be judged by the judgment of human beings was because they kept not their first estate, but left their own habitations for the lust of the flesh? But at any rate these are not Satan and his angels, who have not now to be judged, but are condemned already, and for whom already "everlasting fire is prepared" (Matt. xxv. 41). Some may object to the idea of angels taking wives, &c. &c.; but as Maitland very truly remarks, that act is no more incredible, nor alien to our ideas of a spirit, than that "angels should assume the human form, and eat the calf of Abraham, and the unleavened bread of Lot." Neither does this appear to have staggered the belief of Justin Martyr, Irenæus, Tertullian, Clemens Alexandrinus, &c. Moreover, in the majority of the MSS. of the Septuagint, Gen. iii. 6 stands, οἱ ἄγγελοι τοῦ Θεοῦ, not οἱ υἱοὶ τοῦ Θεοῦ, showing what was then considered to be the meaning of the Hebrew text, that the sons of God meant angels.

Before proceeding further I wish to remark upon another passage in St. Peter's Epistle (1 Pet. iii. 19): "By which also he went and preached unto the spirits in prison, which sometime were disobedient when once the long-suffering of God waited in the days of Noah," &c. The interpretation put upon this passage by Bishop Hall, Archbishop Secker, Bishop Pearson, Calmet, and others, has always appeared to me most unsatisfactory; in substance they say that Christ, by the agency of Noah, preached unto the men of Noah's day, whose spirits being disobedient then, are now in prison; but this is not borne out by the text. If we look back to the 18th verse, we find the order of time in the apostle's statement to be this, 1st, Christ's death, 2nd, his resurrection and his preaching to the spirits in prison, which appear to have occurred at the same period; further, we do not find that he preached to living men, but to spirits (πνεύμασι), to what were spirits when he preached to them. The passage will not bear the construction put upon it, viz., that the preaching was to men *then* on earth, but whose spirits are *now* in prison; the preaching is distinctly stated to have been to " spirits in prison," or imprisoned spirits; and, as our creed holds, St. Peter, in the second chapter of Acts, while illustrating the prophecy of David, shows that our Saviour did descend into Hades, where this preaching must have occurred; but what spirits were they to whom he preached? In this chapter we read that they were those " which sometime were disobedient when once the long-suffering of God waited in the days of Noah;" this marks the time, and clearly refers to Genesis, vi.; but in St. Peter's Second Epistle (chap. ii. verses 4 and 5) we have a similar reference to the preaching of Noah, to the destruction of the world, and to the casting down of sinning angels, who, he says, were imprisoned in Tartarus or Hades; are they not, then, the same spirits (or angels) in prison, to whom Christ, when he descended into Hades, preached? I cannot feel a doubt on the subject, nor do I think that any one who dispassionately lays before his view the sixth chapter of Genesis, the third chapter of the 1st of St. Peter, the second chapter of the 2d of St. Peter, and the Epistle of St. Jude, can arrive at a different conclusion, without strewing his path with insuperable difficulties. Critics generally have found so much difficulty in forcing the passage to bear the construction put upon it (viz., that the preaching was to men then living, but whose spirits were afterwards in prison), that they have been obliged to apologise for its adoption, by showing that the opposite or natural construction of the passage would go far towards sanctioning the doctrine of purgatory, that if Christ preached to the spirits in Hades, then must that preaching have been with a view to their repentance after death. Bishop Horsley disposes of this by showing that the preaching meant probably no more than this, that to the spirits of those who had once been disobedient, but had afterwards repented, Christ preached or proclaimed the fulfilment of the atonement which had been made for them by his death; he cannot bring himself to adopt the idea that the spirits were imprisoned subsequently to the preaching—the apostle's words will not bear it out. So far well; but if, as I hold, the spirits in prison were not the spirits of men, but of angels, who will say that to them, not like men entered upon a different state of being, but still the same in nature as at first, though in chains for judgment,—who will say that to them Christ's preaching might not be the preaching of repentance and faith, a preaching to bear fruits of forgiveness at the last day, when the apostles should "judge angels?" There is a curious passage in Job (xxvi. 5), which, from a defect in the translation, might easily be overlooked as having any bearing upon our subject: in our version it stands thus, "Dead things are formed under the waters," but I believe the better interpretation is, " The giants (*rephaim*) groan or tremble under the waters," *i.e.* in Sheol or Hell, which, according to the belief of the Jews, lay so far below as to be hidden not only under the earth, but under the waters upon which they supposed the earth to stand. Is Job referring to the giants of Genesis vi.? and is the passage one more link of the chain connecting the various passages I have cited, from Genesis to the Epistle of St. Jude? See, also, Ecclesiasticus (xvi. 7), " He was not pacified toward the old giants *who fell away* in the strength of their foolishness, neither spared he the place where Lot sojourned." Here, again, we have a curious illustration of the name given to the giants in Genesis. There we have, in the Hebrew "Nephilim," "the fallen ones," translated in the Septuagint by the word "Gigantes." In Ecclesiasticus we have the two united, the latter paraphrased by the former—" the giants, who fell away" (οἱ ἀπεστήσαν). Now, Ecclesiasticus has no claim to inspiration, but the writer had an accurate knowledge of the Scriptures and of the Hebrew language; and this passage, to my mind, goes far to prove why the giants were called "Nephilim," because they fell away from God. It is, too, a curious coincidence, to say the least, that once again the punishment for the lusts of the flesh in the destruction of Sodom is mentioned in connexion with the punishment of the giants. I do not know that there is much difference of opinion as to the translation of the passage (Jude, 6), Ἀγγέλους τε τοὺς μὴ τηρήσαντας τὴν ἑαυτῶν ἀρχήν, "And the angels which kept not their first estate;" but some, with Dr. Hales, apply it to the Sethites in the age of Enoch. Independently of what I have before maintained, there appears to me to be this critical objection: ἀρχήν, translated "first estate," signifies "birthright," "right of primogeniture," which the angels might have, and which Cain and the Cainites might have, but not the Sethites, the younger branch, when contrasted with the elder. We have the expression in the Septuagint (1 Chron. xxvi. 10), "To Hosah, of the children of Merari, were born sons who were careful to preserve their birthright," υἱοὶ φυλάσσοντες τὴν ἀρχήν. In this case, Hosah's was not a regular primogeniture, for he was not the eldest son, but the argument remains the same, the rights of primogeniture having been given him by his father; but in the case of Seth, the rights of primogeniture were not given, he was "appointed another seed, *instead of Abel,* whom Cain slew" (Gen. iv. 25).

Having now, as I think, seen that those passages supposed to refer to the fall of Satan cannot in reality bear any such construction, being referable either to a subsequent period or to different beings; having endeavoured faithfully to represent popular belief on the subject, and to test it by the Scriptures supposed to be its groundwork; having failed to discover that Satan fell by pride, fell from Heaven, fell at all, or was ever other than he is; it remains to us carefully to carry out the fourth proposition by collating such texts as appear to throw light on the subject, and to ascertain the history, nature, station, pursuits, power, and destiny of the Devil, so far as revealed to us in Scripture. In doing this we must not expect a very clear revelation of Satan's history, nor having pointed out the error of popular ideas, hope to substitute anything equally connected in their place.

No sooner had man come pure and sinless from his Maker's hand, than we find (Gen. iii. 1) a power adverse to God and hostile to man, marring God's work by seducing him from obedience. This power is called "the serpent." "Now the serpent was more subtile than any beast of the field," &c. but St. John tells us (Rev. xii. 9), that "that old serpent is called the Devil and Satan." Why the Devil assumed the form of a serpent, we are not told; but such was his first introduction to our race; in this form was he cursed by God (Gen. iii. 14, 15), and while in this semblance God said the woman's seed should bruise his head, and he should bruise his heel. This was the first introduction of Satan to our race, and the first time also that he is mentioned in Scripture. Throughout the sacred pages he is called by many different titles, but "Satan" and "the Devil" are the most frequent and the most peculiarly his own. The signification of either is familiar to every one, διάβολος, the calumniator, or accuser, being nearly a literal translation of the Hebrew "Sathanas," an adversary, or accuser in a court of justice. In the narrative of the fall, we have no information as to the nature of Satan or his motives, the bare facts only implying enmity to man, opposition to God. He is not spoken of as a fallen angel, nor, though cursed by God, was he subjected to everlasting chains and imprisonment, as were the angels who fell after this time (Gen. vi. 2, and Jude, verse 6.) By and bye we find him presenting himself before God (Job, i. 6): "Now there was a day when the sons of God came to present themselves before the Lord, and Satan came also among them. And the Lord said unto Satan, Whence comest thou? Then Satan answered the Lord, and said, From going to and fro in the earth, and from walking up and down in it." There is nothing here to induce us to suppose that though Satan came among the sons of God (the angels), that he also was a son of God, *i.e.* an angel, a fallen angel. From his manner, from his actions, from the treatment he meets with, he might have been an evil spirit from the first. There is nothing in the narrative to suggest any other supposition; neither, so far as we can judge, is it more unlikely there should have been *an evil spirit* from the first, than that there should have been *a spirit of evil*, and this there must have been if a pure angel sinned. While opposing God, Satan is perfectly conscious of his impotence against God; he seeks *permission* to tempt God's servant (Job, i. 9, 10, 11), showing that without God's permission he cannot hurt us. Again, in the second chapter (verse 5), he seeks further license to tempt Job, not only in his goods and children, but in his flesh and bones. When Cain murdered Abel the Devil was his instigator, for St. John says (1 John, iii. 12), "he was of that wicked one." In (1 Chron. xxi. 1), "Satan provoked David to number Israel." In Zechariah (iii. 1), "He showed me Joshua the high-priest standing before the Angel of the Lord, and Satan standing at his right hand to resist him." Here, again, where we find the Angel of God to aid, we find also the Devil to resist. So it ever is and has been, as we may read throughout the pages of the Bible, and in the daily experience of the world. In all cases he opposes himself to God, knowing his inferiority, but asserting his independence. It seems probable that the Magicians of Egypt had their power from the Devil. They acted in opposition to Moses whom God sent to exhibit His miracles before Pharaoh, and therefore it is clear they had not their power from God, yet their power was more than human; whence then could it come but from the prince of this world, the Devil? So, also, may we conclude, the witch of Endor and all witches derived their power from the Devil; and in the Apostles' time St. Paul calls the sorcerer Elymas "a child of the Devil." (Acts, xiii. 10.) The damsel at Thyatira (Acts, xvi. 16) had a spirit of divination, which Paul commanded to come out of her in the name of Jesus Christ. Was not her power of Satan? Such also was the power of Simon Magus (Acts, viii. 9), but in fact, from one end of the Bible to the other, the direct influence of Satan upon mankind is fully recognised. He granted to men supernatural powers, he filled their minds with evil inclinations, he took possession of their living bodies, produced madness, (Mark, v. 2), and (Matt. xvii. 15) inflicted disease, as in the case of the infirm woman, whom Satan had bound eighteen years (Luke, xiii. 16). Nay, so general does the evil power of Satan appear, and so various are the evils and diseases, mental and bodily, which are attributed to him, that it becomes a question how far we may be justified in supposing that all disease is, by God's permission, the direct infliction of Satan. The more narrowly we search, the more deeply we ponder, the more difficult we shall find it to believe that such power should be accorded to a rebellious servant, an apostate angel; that Almighty God should (contrary to His dealings with other fallen angels) allow a rebellious servant so to corrupt God's own creation, that millions of His creatures should actually transfer their allegiance to Satan, and that those who ultimately attain the Kingdom of God, attain it only by the atoning sacrifice of God's own Son; while the world of His creation, which was pronounced "good" as it came from God's hand, has been polluted and disfigured by Satan, till the fervent heat of fire alone can purify it. To what, then, do these observations tend? If Satan was not originally an Angel of Light, what was he? And if his fall was not the origin of evil, what was? I do not say that *from Scripture* it is possible, and if not *so* possible, certainly not necessary, that man should be able to solve the mysterious problem of the origin of evil. God is good and true, holy and just, and the Bible is God's word. Whatever, therefore, we find there written *of God* we are by faith to receive as true and good, and holy and just, though we may not always be able to reconcile it with our imperfect ideas on the subject; but, on the other hand, we are not to exaggerate the difficulties of revelation in order that we may exhibit the fulness of our faith; for example, if the Bible reveal to us that Satan originally came from the hand of God a pure and holy angel, that from being pure and holy, enjoying the presence and favour of God, without temptation from without or impurity within, he nevertheless fell into the depths of wickedness, the avowed enemy of God, the ruthless destroyer of the souls of God's creatures;—if, I say, we find this revealed to us, then "let God be true, and every man a liar," we must believe the imperfection is of us, not of God; but is this revealed? Where? When? Was Satan ever a good angel? Did he ever fall? Was he ever other than he is now? If there be no proof, direct or indirect, by assertion or by implication, then are we not only at liberty, but it is our bounden duty to ascertain what God has revealed to us on the subject; and if in the investigation a theory of the origin of evil should present itself, we shall not be obliged to cast it aside because it is at variance with the received notions about Satan,—those notions being unfounded in Scripture. Let me not be met with the objection that the ideas I suggest have been mixed up with the doctrines of this or that heretic who has been duly condemned by the councils of his time. What errors have not been sanctioned? what truth has not been impugned at one time or other, by the same authority? But we need have no difficulty on this point, we have the same guide to refer to as that to which the councils were amenable. On the Bible I base my arguments, and by the Bible revelation their truth must stand or fall.

Supposing the Bible to be silent on the subject, I confess it appears to me not only as likely, but infinitely more likely, that the Devil has existed from eternity as an evil spirit, than that having been once good he fell from Heaven. Nothing can be more revolting to our ideas of probability,

I may almost say of possibility, than that such a fall should happen. Can we conceive it possible that even man, lower far in the scale of creation than the Devil is supposed to have been,—can we suppose that even man would have fallen *untempted?* Still less, then, would an angel with far higher and clearer perceptions of God's goodness and power, with far keener spiritual enjoyment and satisfaction in the glories of Heaven, have fallen *untempted;* and where was his tempter? "God tempts no man," and we may safely add, God tempts no angel. But suppose for a moment (for the sake of argument only) a good angel to have fallen; do we, assuming this, find ourselves in a position to reconcile this fall of Satan with what God has actually revealed to us of the position of Satan, not only in relation to man, but to the great God Himself? Is it a natural or probable sequence because Satan rebelled against his God and fell, that God should thenceforward constitute him "the God of this world" (2 Cor. iv. 4), "the Prince of the power of the air" (Eph. ii. 2), "the Prince of Darkness" (Eph. vi. 12), that he should leave him at liberty to sully the purity, subvert the allegiance, change the destiny of God's new creatures—man—that he should enable him by extraordinary spiritual and physical powers and manifestations, to secure to himself the worship and fealty of man, which was due to God alone; that he should so entirely and absolutely, not in name merely, become "the Prince of this world," as to presume to tempt our blessed Lord Himself, and offer to Him a transfer of the kingdoms of the world. Surely this is not the power and condition of a fallen angel, however great! Surely a fallen angel, however great, could not have rendered necessary the mysterious sacrifice of God's own and only Son, before we could be rescued from destruction and redeemed from the dominion of the Devil! But once more let me not be misunderstood; if Scripture assert that Christ died to save us from the power of His apostate servant, we must believe it without hesitation; but if Scripture assert nothing of the kind, are we not at liberty to say that, first, it is an incredible thing a pure and good angel should spontaneously fall; secondly, that falling he should be placed in a position of terrible power in reference to the rest of God's creation, with legions of evil angels to do his bidding; thirdly, that it should be necessary, in order to counteract the wickedness of an apostate servant, that God Himself in the person of His Son should become man, and die upon the cross, and even thus recover but a small portion of the human race,—even thus leave the greater part of mankind the victims and subjects of Satan? Does not even the mysterious sacrifice of Christ become more intelligible if we look upon Satan as an independent power, an evil spirit existent from eternity, existent when the earth was chaos and confusion, and darkness was upon the face of the deep?

Let us once again return to Scripture, and ascertain first, Is this idea contrary to the Bible?

If not, then further, is it in any way *directly* supported by Scripture? But before examining this point, I would take for what it is worth the testimony of ancient philosophers, and the consent of heathen nations. Plutarch assures us, it was the belief of philosophers that there were from the beginning two spirits, a spirit of good and a spirit of evil. There can be no doubt but that this idea is generally diffused among heathen nations in the present day; and we may argue from it, that as they received their ideas of a creation, a deluge, and other matters, by tradition, more or less correct, of real facts, so is there a probability that their tradition of a spirit of evil, no less than of a spirit of good, existent from eternity, had its origin in truth also. This much for heathen testimony. I now return to Scripture. Is the idea contrary to Scripture? We have already seen that it is not. It occurs to me, however, to notice one or two passages, which might be adduced as apparently opposed to my views. Take, for instance, Colossians (i. 16), "For by him were all things created that are in heaven, and that are in earth, visible and invisible, whether they be thrones, or dominions, or principalities, or powers—all things were created by him and for him." Taking this passage alone, where God is said to have created "all things" ($\pi\acute{a}\nu\tau\alpha$), and even $\pi\acute{a}\nu\tau\alpha$ amplified, if possible, by the context, I should have concluded that Satan and his host must have been included; but let me not be considered captious or hypercritical if I limit the creation mentioned to "things in heaven and things on earth;" if I exclude Satan and his host from this creation, I do so to avoid a more serious difficulty which will otherwise beset us,—if we continue the chapter to the 20th verse, where we read that the same πάντα in heaven and earth are to be *reconciled to God*. This proves that πάντα cannot include the Devil, who is not to be reconciled to God. But take St. John's Gospel, chap. i., "All things were made by Him, and without Him was not anything made *that was made*." This limitation may or may not have a meaning; I do not wish to build too much upon it. Again, it has been argued that Satan was at one time *good*, because we read, "He abode not in the truth." At first sight, and taken alone, it might seem to imply that he was in the truth once; but does it really mean this? The passage runs thus, "He was a murderer *from the beginning*, and stood not in the truth." This must have been from the beginning also; or are we to suppose that though he was a murderer from the beginning, yet that he regarded the truth once even when he was a murderer, and that it was only afterwards that he ceased to abide in it? But it requires not this argument; the simple meaning appears to be, that to ruin our first parents he told falsehoods, because the truth was not in him, and that the Jews believe not the truth, because they prefer the falsehood of the Devil. In Isaiah (xlv. 7) we have this expression, "I make peace and I create evil;" but surely Lowth and others, supposing it intended as a refutation of the Magian doctrine of a good spirit and an evil spirit, then prevalent, have erred in interpreting this to mean that *wickedness* was of God's creation. Must we not rather interpret it to signify *the evil of punishment*, which there can be no doubt God exercises on the heads of sinners, either directly, or by evil spirits acting by his permission. What says Job (ii. 10)? " Shall we receive good at the hand of God, and shall we not receive evil?" *i. e.* the evil of punishment. Again, Amos (iii. 6), "Shall there be evil in the city, and the Lord hath not done it?" and in other passages without number; but the very idea of evil, as meaning sin and the Devil, being of God's creation, has to my mind the impress of profanation upon it. Our Saviour refutes the imputation of Satanic agency in his miracles by the simile of a house divided against a house, "How shall it stand?" But surely it would be not less applicable to God's house if God created sin and Satan to mar the beauty of His structure! Can these things be?

But, to proceed: Is the view I am advocating directly supported by Scripture? I think it is. In the First Epistle of St. John (chap. iii. verse 8), we read, " The devil sinneth from the beginning." It has been said that this means from the beginning of our world, but why? I take it rather to mean from eternity, just as in St. John's Gospel (i. 1) we read, " In the beginning (*i. e.* from eternity) was the Word." The same Greek word $\dot{\alpha}\rho\chi\dot{\eta}$ is used in both places, as also in St. John (i. 2, 13), " Ye have known him which is from the beginning," and this is one of the passages always insisted upon as proving the pre-existence of Christ: ἀρχή always appears to be used to indicate the earliest time applicable to the subject in hand; it is one end of a thing, the beginning of time, *i. e.* eternity; the beginning of the world, the beginning of the Gospel dispensation, &c., according to the requirements of the subject in hand. In St. John (chap. viii. 44), our Saviour says, "Satan was a manslayer, ἀπ' ἀρχῆς, from the beginning;" a murderer, either in disposition, from his own beginning, or, in fact, from the beginning of the human race, the earliest period when he could be so. So also in many other passages, but when St. John says, "He sinneth from the beginning," there is nothing in the subject that should lead us to suppose the beginning of this world to be intended; on the contrary, we may fairly conclude that when used exactly in a similar manner to that in which it is used in reference to Christ, we are justified in assigning to it the same signification; we are justified, perhaps, in supposing that when "in the beginning God created the heavens and the earth," that chaos, confusion, and darkness, were the work of the Devil.

The subject is one on which human speculation can prove nothing, reason falters, judgment avails us not. Milton has made him a creature; Shakspere has called him "Eternal." I cannot accept the doctrine from either, though the former appears to have blinded the judgment of most men, substituting Pagan myths and German mysticisms for Bible revelations.

Having now, however imperfectly, fulfilled the purpose with which I set forth, I must leave it to others either to disprove from Scripture the arguments I have adduced, or to confirm those arguments by further elucidation. In either case I may humbly hope that good, and not evil, must result from a conscientious endeavour to ascertain what is, and what is not, revealed to us in Holy Writ; my belief is that a history has been composed, and an edifice raised, without foundation; I cannot find it in the Bible; but instead I find scattered fragments of another building, too few to compose a uniform structure, but too many and too important to remain neglected. But whatever be the conclusion to which we come, of one thing let us beware. The existence of sin, and the toleration of it by God, has impressed many great minds with the idea of a limitation of God's power, but this is not less opposed to reason than to revelation. God's ways are not as our ways, neither by searching can we find them out; and whether Satan be a fallen creature or an evil essence, revelation not only declares God's power, but also His will, at His own time to vanquish both sin and Satan. Reason may cavil at the delay, but cannot deny the omnipotence of the act, and must admit that God's toleration of sin for a season is self-imposed, and not from external necessity.

Printed by Libri Plureos GmbH in Hamburg,
Germany